Apes
Find
Shapes

by Jane Belk Moncure
illustrated by Joy Friedman

Published by

Mankato, Minnesota

The Library —
A Magic Castle

Come to the magic castle
When you are growing tall.
Rows upon rows of Word Windows
Line every single wall.
They reach up high,
As high as the sky,
And you want to open them all.
For every time you open one,
A new adventure has begun.

Tracy opens a Word Window.

Guess what Tracy sees?

Four
funny
apes.

"Hi," say the apes.
"Let's find shapes."

"This is an ape in a shape,
in a circle shape,"

says the first little ape. "Let's find
circle shapes."

The apes find
traffic light circles—
one, two, three—

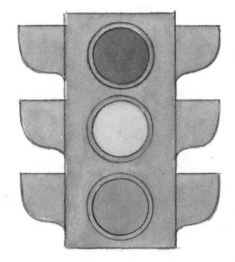

and circle eyes
on an owl
in a tree.

9

They find round circle pancakes,
cooking in a pan,

bubbles, a ball, and a circle snowman.

"Let's eat a circle," says the ape.
"Let's do."

Tracy eats one donut.
The ape eats two.

"This is a square shape," says the

second little ape.

"Let's find square shapes."

They find a
square window

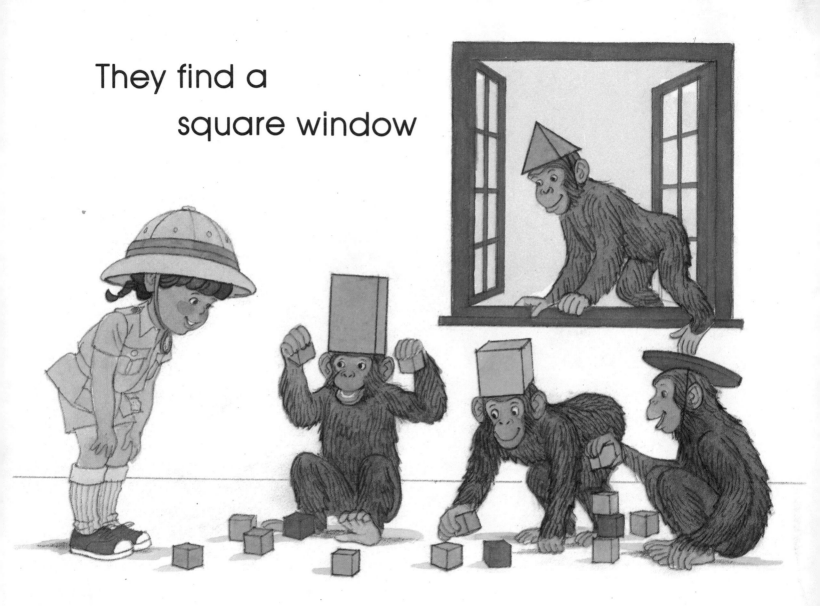

and little square blocks,

14

a checkerboard

and a big, square box.

They find

stickers

and books

and a lunch box too—

and then a lion's square cage

at the zoo.

"Let's eat a square," says the ape.
"Let's do."

Tracy eats one cracker.
The ape eats two.

"This is a triangle shape," says the

third little ape.

"Let's find triangle shapes."

They find triangle flags

and a
triangle
sail . . .

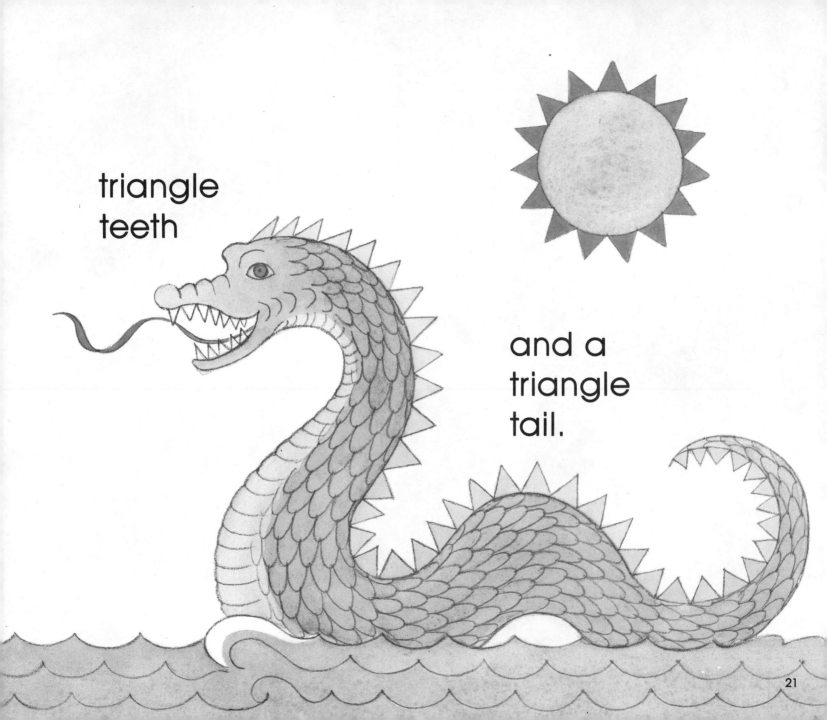

triangle
teeth

and a
triangle
tail.

21

They find . . .

triangle  baskets

and a little tepee . . .

a triangle kite

and a
triangle tree.

"Let's eat a triangle," says the ape.
"Let's do."

Tracy eats one slice of pie.
The ape eats two.

"This is a rectangle shape," says the

fourth
little
ape.

"Let's find
rectangle
shapes."

They find
rectangle
windows,

a rectangle
door,

and a
rectangle
robot

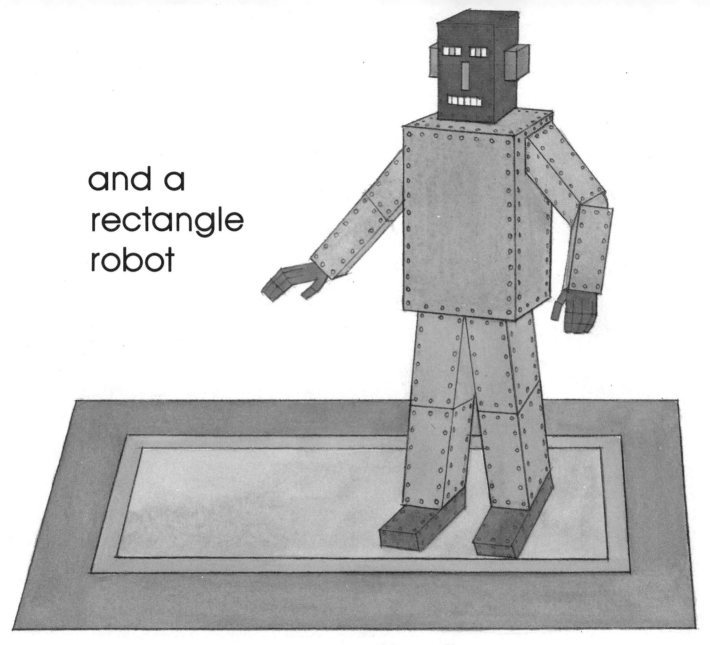

on a rug on the floor.

"Let's eat a rectangle," says the ape.
"Let's do."

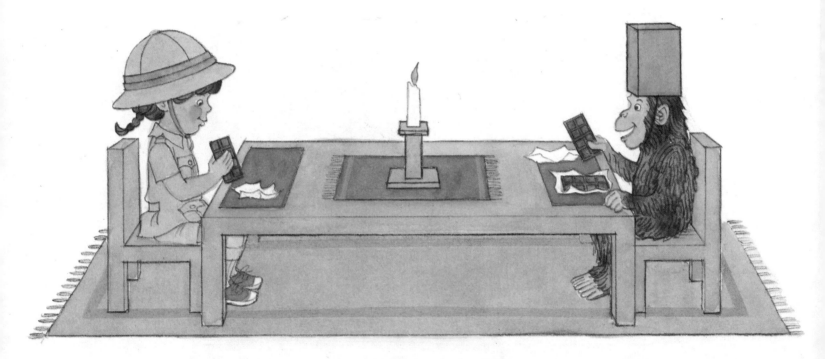

Tracy eats one candy bar.
The ape eats two.

Then four little apes
put shapes together

and zoom
away.

"Bye-bye."

Tracy closes the Word Window.

Can you read these words with Tracy?

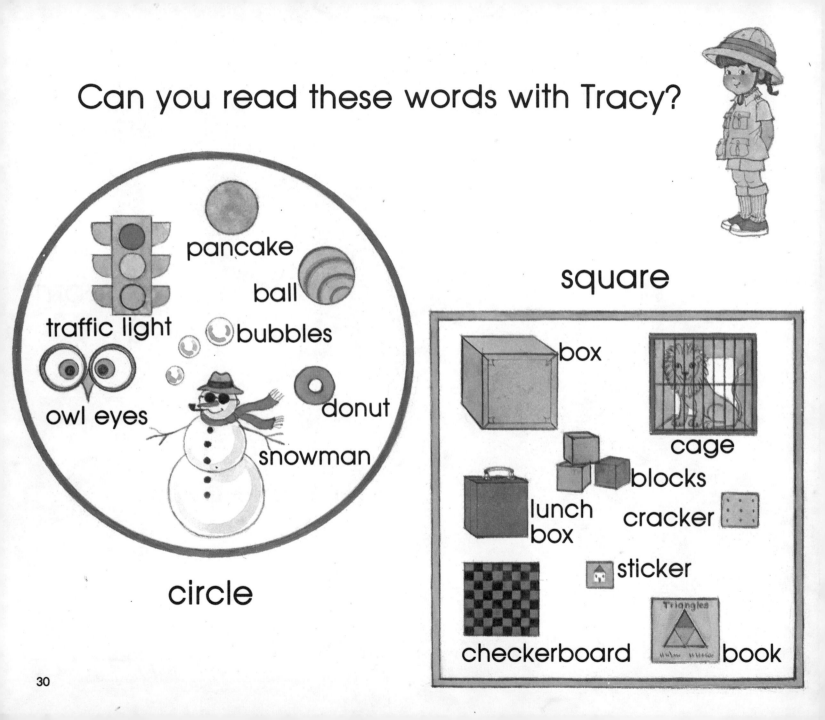

circle
- pancake
- ball
- traffic light
- bubbles
- owl eyes
- donut
- snowman

square
- box
- cage
- blocks
- lunch box
- cracker
- sticker
- checkerboard
- book